How to Shoot Photos and Videos with Canon EOS R6 Mark III Like a Pro

Camera Settings, Composition, Lighting, and Real-World Techniques for Stunning Results

Sammy Addy

How to Shoot Photos and Videos with Canon EOS R6 Mark III Like a Pro 1

Master Camera Settings, Composition, Lighting, and Real-World Techniques for Stunning Results   1

Disclaimer   5

Introduction   6

Chapter 1   6

Video Recording on the R6 Mark III   6

  Switching to video mode   6

  Video menu layout   8

  How the menu changes in video mode   9

  Resolution and frame rate   13

  Autofocus in video   17

  Audio settings   23

  Microphone setup   28

  Overheating considerations   33

  Beginner video settings   38

Chapter 2   43

Connectivity and Wireless Features   43

  Bluetooth pairing   47

  Step 4: Confirm pairing on the camera   53

  Using Canon apps   55

  Installing the Canon Camera Connect app   56

  Transferring photos and videos   61

  Remote shooting   65

Chapter 3   71

Customization and Personal Setup   71

  Button customization   71

  Opening button customization (step by step)   72

  Custom shooting modes   75

  My Menu setup   80

  Saving preferred settings   85

Chapter 4   90

Maintenance and Care   90

  Cleaning the camera body   90

Chapter 5   95

Common Problems and Simple Fixes   95

  Camera won't turn on   95

Disclaimer

This book, *How to Shoot Photos and Videos with Canon R6 Mark III Like a Pro: Camera Settings*, Composition, lighting, Real-world Techniques for Stunning Techniques is an **independent educational guide** created to help users understand and operate the Canon EOS R6 Mark III camera.

This book is **not affiliated with, endorsed by, sponsored by, or approved by Canon Inc.** or any of its subsidiaries. Canon®, EOS®, and all related names, logos, and trademarks are the property of their respective owners and are used in this book **solely for identification and instructional purposes**.

The information provided in this book is based on practical use, research, and user experience. While every effort has been made to ensure accuracy and clarity, camera firmware updates, settings options, or operational behavior may change over time. The author and publisher **do not guarantee that all information will remain current or error-free**.

This book is intended for **educational purposes only**. The author and publisher shall not be held responsible for any damage to equipment, data loss, personal injury, or other issues resulting from the use or misuse of information contained in this book. Readers are encouraged to follow official safety instructions provided by the manufacturer and to use the camera responsibly.

By using this book, the reader acknowledges that **all camera operation decisions are made at their own discretion and risk**.

Introduction
Chapter 1

Video Recording on the R6 Mark III

Switching to video mode

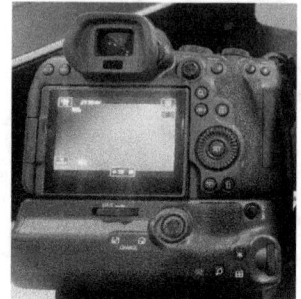

On the Canon EOS R6 Mark III, video recording is enabled by **switching the camera into Movie (video) mode**. This is a physical action combined with on-screen confirmation. Until the camera is in video mode, it will behave as a stills camera even if you press the record button.

This section explains **exactly where video mode is**, **how to switch to it**, and **what changes on the camera when you do**, step by step.

Where video mode is located on the camera

Video mode is controlled using the **Mode Dial on** the **top of the camera**.

The Mode Dial is located on the **top-right area** of the camera body

It is the large rotating dial with letters and symbols

One of the positions is marked with a **movie camera icon**

This icon represents **Movie (video) mode**

How to switch to video mode (step by step)

Turn the camera ON using the power switch

Place your right hand on the camera grip

Use your index finger and thumb to rotate the **Mode Dial**

Turn the dial until the **movie camera icon** lines up with the indicator mark

Release the dial

Photos and Videos Like a Pro

The camera is now in video mode.

What changes immediately when you enter video mode
Once video mode is active:

    The screen switches to a **video-specific display**

    Video frame guides may appear

    Video resolution and frame rate indicators appear

    Exposure behavior adapts for video

    Photo-only options are hidden

    Video menus become available

This confirms the camera is no longer in photo mode.

How to confirm you are in video mode
You can confirm video mode in three ways:

    The **movie camera icon** is visible on screen

    Video-specific information (frame rate, recording format) is displayed

    Pressing the shutter button does **not** take a photo

If pressing the shutter still takes a photo, the camera is not in video mode.

What the shutter button does in video mode
In video mode:

    The shutter button **does not record video**

    It may still be used for:

        Autofocus activation

        Exposure metering

    Video recording is started using the **Record (video) button**

This separation prevents accidental recordings.

What settings are remembered separately for video

Important camera-specific behavior:

Video mode has its **own settings**

Exposure, ISO, Picture Style, and AF settings can differ from photo mode

Changing settings in video mode does not affect photo mode

This allows you to set up the camera differently for video and photos.

Common beginner mistakes when switching to video mode

Pressing the record button while still in photo mode

Forgetting to rotate the Mode Dial fully

Expecting photo settings to carry over

Thinking the camera is recording when it is not

Always confirm the movie icon before recording.

Best practice for beginners

Always switch to video mode before recording

Confirm video indicators on screen

Set up exposure and AF after entering video mode

Do not rely on photo mode settings

Practice switching modes slowly and deliberately

Switching to video mode on the Canon EOS R6 Mark III is a **physical, intentional step** that unlocks all video features and prevents accidental recordings.

Video menu layout

When the Canon EOS R6 Mark III is switched to **video mode**, the MENU system changes. Photo-only options are hidden, and **video-specific menus appear**. Understanding this layout is important because many video problems beginners face come from changing the wrong menu or not realizing they are still in the photo menu.

This section explains **how the video menu is laid out, what changes when you enter video mode**, and **how to move through video menus correctly**, step by step.

How the menu changes in video mode

Once the Mode Dial is set to the **movie camera icon** and you press **MENU**:

   The menu switches to **movie-focused pages**

   Shooting settings are now video-based

   Some photo-only items disappear

   New video-only items appear

This confirms you are working inside the video system, not the photo system.

The color-coded tabs in video mode

The video menu still uses Canon's familiar color system, but the **content inside each tab changes**.

You will typically see:

Red tab (Movie Shooting Menu)

Purple tab (Autofocus Menu)

Blue tab (Playback Menu)

Yellow tab (Setup Menu)

Green tab (My Menu)

Even though the colors are the same, the **Red tab now controls video settings**, not photo settings.

Red tab in video mode (Movie Shooting Menu)

Photos and Videos Like a Pro

This is the most important tab for video.

Inside this tab, you will find:

- Movie recording quality (resolution and frame rate)

- Movie file format

- HDR or special video modes (if enabled)

- Time limits and recording behavior

- Exposure-related video settings

- Video stabilization options

Everything in this tab affects **how your video is recorded**, not still photos.

If you do not see movie-related options, you are not in video mode.

Purple tab in video mode (Autofocus Menu)
This tab controls **how autofocus behaves during video recording**.

You will find options such as:

- AF operation for video

- Subject detection for video

- Eye detection behavior in video

- AF tracking sensitivity

- Touch AF settings

Changes made here affect **video AF only**, not photo AF.

Blue tab in video mode (Playback Menu)
This tab controls how recorded videos are reviewed.

You will find:

- Playback options for movies

- Display information during playback

- Jump and review behavior

This tab does not affect recording quality.

Yellow tab in video mode (Setup Menu)

This tab controls general camera behavior that applies to video.

You may find:

Card recording options

Power saving settings

HDMI output behavior

Date, time, and language

Screen brightness and display settings

Some settings here affect both photo and video.

Green tab in video mode (My Menu)

This tab allows you to:

Add frequently used video menu items

Create a custom shortcut menu for video

Quickly access recording quality, AF, or audio settings

My Menu can be set up differently for video than for photos.

How video menu pages are organized

Within each tab:

Settings are divided into multiple pages

Page numbers appear at the top or bottom

Use the **Main Dial** or **Rear Dial** to move between pages

Use the **Joystick** to move between items

The camera remembers the last menu page used.

How to move safely inside the video menu

Step-by-step navigation:

Photos and Videos Like a Pro

Press **MENU**

Confirm you see movie-related options

Use the **Main Dial** to move between tabs

Use the **Rear Dial** to change pages

Use the **Joystick** to select items

Press **SET** to enter a setting

Press **MENU** or half-press the shutter to exit

How to know you are adjusting video settings, not photo settings

Always confirm:

The **movie camera icon** is visible on screen

Menu items mention "Movie" or "Video"

Recording quality shows frame rates (like 24p, 30p, 60p)

If you see photo resolution or still image options, exit and recheck the

Mode Dial.

Common beginner mistakes with the video menu

Changing photo menu settings while thinking they affect video

Forgetting to switch to video mode before opening MENU

Adjusting the wrong tab

Not noticing that video and photo menus are separate

Expecting photo Picture Styles to behave the same as video

Best practice for beginners

Always switch to video mode first

Press MENU only after confirming movie mode

Start all video setup from the **Red Movie Shooting tab**

Make small changes and test recording

Use My Menu to store important video settings

Exit the menu and record a short clip to confirm changes

The video menu layout on the Canon EOS R6 Mark III is **logical and separated** once you understand that video mode has its own menu system. Knowing this prevents confusion and ensures every change you make actually affects your video.

Resolution and frame rate

On the Canon EOS R6 Mark III, **resolution and frame rate control how your video looks and how smoothly motion is recorded**. These settings are adjusted together from one specific location in the video menu. If you change resolution or frame rate, you are changing how the camera records video at a fundamental level.

This section explains **exactly where these settings are**, **how to change them**, and **what each option means on this camera**, step by step, in simple language.

Where resolution and frame rate are located

Resolution and frame rate are found in the **Movie Shooting Menu**, which is the **Red tab when the camera is in video mode**.

You must be in **video mode** to see these options.

Step-by-step: opening the resolution and frame rate menu

Turn the camera ON

Rotate the **Mode Dial** to the **movie camera icon**

Press the **MENU** button

Confirm you are in the **Red Movie Shooting tab**

Select **Movie recording quality**

Press **SET**

You are now on the screen where resolution and frame rate are chosen.

How the Movie recording quality screen is laid out
On this screen, you will see:

Resolution options (for example, 4K or Full HD)

Frame rate options (for example, 24p, 30p, 60p)

A combined format label showing both values together

You do not set resolution and frame rate separately. You select a **combined option**.

Understanding resolution options on the R6 Mark III
Resolution controls **how detailed the video image is**.

Common options you may see:

4K

Very high detail

Larger file sizes

More demanding on memory cards

Best for high-quality video and future-proofing

Full HD (1080p)

Lower resolution than 4K

Smaller file sizes

Easier to edit

Good for everyday video

What to know:

Higher resolution does not mean better exposure or color

It only affects image detail and file size

Understanding frame rate options on this camera

Frame rate controls **how many frames are recorded per second**.

Common frame rate values you may see:

24p

    Cinematic motion

    Slightly less smooth movement

    Common for storytelling and films

30p

    Natural, standard motion

    Good for general video

    Looks smooth on most screens

60p

    Very smooth motion

    Useful for fast movement

    Allows slow motion in editing

Higher frame rates:

    Increase file size

    Require faster memory cards

    Reduce recording time per card

How to select a resolution and frame rate

Step-by-step:

    Inside **Movie recording quality**

    Use the **joystick** to highlight a resolution/frame rate option

    Watch the description update on screen

    Press **SET** to confirm

Exit the menu

The selected setting becomes active immediately.

How to confirm the active resolution and frame rate
On the video shooting screen:

Look for resolution and frame rate text (for example, 4K 30p)

This appears on the LCD and in the viewfinder

It stays visible while recording

Always confirm this before pressing record.

How resolution and frame rate affect recording time
Camera-specific behavior:

Higher resolution = shorter recording time

Higher frame rate = shorter recording time

Memory cards fill faster at higher settings

If recording stops unexpectedly:

Check card speed

Check remaining card space

Check recording format

Resolution and frame rate in relation to heat and performance
Important beginner note:

Higher video settings demand more processing

Long recordings at high resolution may generate heat

The camera manages this automatically

If the camera limits recording:

Reduce resolution or frame rate

Allow the camera to cool

How resolution and frame rate affect autofocus and stabilization

On the R6 Mark III:

Autofocus works in all supported video modes

Subject detection remains active

Stabilization behavior may vary slightly with resolution

The camera adjusts internally to maintain performance.

Common beginner mistakes

Forgetting to switch to video mode before changing settings

Recording in 4K when Full HD is sufficient

Using high frame rate unnecessarily

Not checking available card space

Expecting frame rate to change brightness

Best practice for beginners

Start with **Full HD 30p** for learning

Use **4K 30p** when quality matters

Use **60p** only for fast motion or slow motion plans

Always confirm the setting before recording

Test a short clip after changing resolution

On the Canon EOS R6 Mark III, resolution and frame rate are **central video controls**. Once you know exactly where they are and how they affect recording, you can choose settings confidently instead of guessing.

Autofocus in video

Autofocus in video on the Canon EOS R6 Mark III is **always active and continuous by design**. Unlike still photos where focus may lock and stop, video autofocus is meant to **track subjects smoothly while recording**. This section explains **where video AF settings are**, **how to turn them on**, **how to control them**, and **how they behave specifically on this camera**, step by step.

Where video autofocus settings are located

All video autofocus settings are found in the **Purple Autofocus tab**, but **only when the camera is in video mode**.

If you do not see movie-related AF options, the camera is not in video mode.

Step-by-step: accessing video autofocus settings

Turn the camera ON

Rotate the **Mode Dial** to the **movie camera icon**

Press the **MENU** button

Navigate to the **Purple Autofocus tab**

You are now inside the video autofocus control area.

AF operation in video

This is the most important autofocus setting for video.

How to find it:

In the Purple Autofocus tab

Select **AF operation**

Press **SET**

You will see autofocus options for video.

How it works on the R6 Mark III:

Movie Servo AF is the primary mode

Autofocus continuously adjusts while recording

Focus does not lock unless you stop AF manually

How to enable it:

> Highlight **Movie Servo AF**
>
> Set it to **Enable**
>
> Press **SET**

Movie Servo AF should remain enabled for most video use.

Subject detection in video

The R6 Mark III allows subject-based autofocus in video.

How to access it:

> In the Purple Autofocus tab
>
> Select **Subject to detect**
>
> Press **SET**

Available subject options may include:

> People
>
> Animals
>
> Vehicles
>
> None

What happens:

> The camera looks for the selected subject type
>
> It prioritizes that subject during video
>
> Tracking boxes appear on screen

Beginner advice:

> Use **People** for vlogs and interviews
>
> Use **Animals** for pets or wildlife
>
> Use **None** for general scenes

Eye detection in video

Photos and Videos Like a Pro

Eye detection works in video when People or Animals are selected.

How to enable Eye AF:

Go to **Eye detection**

Set it to **Enable**

Press **SET**

What you will see:

A small box over the eye

The box moves as the subject moves

Focus stays on the eye while recording

This is extremely useful for face-to-camera video.

AF area selection for video
This controls **where the camera is allowed to focus**.

How to find it:

In the Purple Autofocus tab

Select **AF area**

Press **SET**

Common options include:

Whole area AF

Zone AF

Spot AF

How it behaves in video:

Whole area AF lets the camera decide

Zone AF limits focus to part of the frame

Spot AF focuses only where you place the point

Beginner recommendation:

Use **Whole area AF** with subject detection enabled

Using Touch AF in video

Touch AF is very important in video.

How to use it:

Make sure **Touch AF** is enabled in the AF menu

While recording or before recording

Tap a subject on the LCD screen

What happens:

The camera smoothly shifts focus to the tapped subject

Focus transition is gradual, not sudden

Tracking continues after the tap

This allows you to control focus without touching buttons.

AF speed and tracking sensitivity (video-specific)

The R6 Mark III allows you to control how autofocus behaves during video.

Where to find it:

Purple Autofocus tab

Look for **Movie AF speed**

Look for **AF tracking sensitivity**

Movie AF speed:

Controls how fast focus transitions

Slower speed = smoother focus pulls

Faster speed = quicker refocus

AF tracking sensitivity:

Controls how easily focus switches to new subjects

Lower sensitivity = stays locked

Higher sensitivity = switches quickly

Beginner advice:

Use default values at first

Adjust only after watching recorded footage

How autofocus behaves while recording

Important camera-specific behavior:

Autofocus continues during recording

Subject detection stays active

Exposure and focus work together

AF does not pause unless disabled

If focus hunts:

Reduce tracking sensitivity

Use a clearer subject

Improve lighting

How to temporarily stop autofocus during video

If you want to stop focus movement:

Switch the lens to **MF**

Or disable Movie Servo AF

This freezes focus where it is.

Common beginner mistakes with video autofocus

Forgetting to enable Movie Servo AF

Using Spot AF and missing focus

Touching the screen accidentally

Expecting focus to lock automatically

Changing AF settings in photo mode instead of video mode

Photos and Videos Like a Pro

Best practice for beginners

Always enable **Movie Servo AF**

Use **Whole area AF**

Enable **Subject detection**

Enable **Eye detection**

Use Touch AF for control

Test focus behavior before recording long clips

Autofocus in video on the Canon EOS R6 Mark III is **powerful, intelligent, and smooth** when set correctly. Once you know where the settings are and how they behave, the camera does most of the work for you.

Audio settings

Audio on the Canon EOS R6 Mark III is controlled **entirely from the video menu** when the camera is in **video mode**. If audio sounds poor, distorted, or silent, the issue is almost always in this menu. This section explains **where audio settings are, how to adjust them,** and **how they behave on this camera**, step by step, in simple language.

Where audio settings are located

All audio controls are found in the **Red Movie Shooting tab**, but **only when the camera is in video mode**.

If you are in photo mode, audio settings will not appear.

Step-by-step: opening the audio settings menu

Turn the camera ON

Rotate the **Mode Dial** to the **movie camera icon**

Press the **MENU** button

Go to the **Red Movie Shooting tab**

Scroll until you find **Sound recording**

Press **SET**

You are now inside the audio control screen.

Sound recording: On or Off
This is the master audio switch.

Inside **Sound recording**, you will see:

Enable

Disable

How to set it:

Highlight **Sound recording**

Set it to **Enable**

Press **SET**

If this is set to Disable:

No audio is recorded

Microphones will not work

The video will be silent .

Always confirm this first.

Audio recording mode: Auto vs Manual
The R6 Mark III allows two audio control modes.

How to find it:

Inside the **Sound recording** menu

Auto audio:

The camera adjusts audio levels automatically

Good for beginners

Levels may rise and fall during recording

Photos and Videos Like a Pro

Manual audio:

    You control the microphone level yourself

    More consistent sound

    Preferred for serious video work

Beginner recommendation:

    Start with **Auto**

    Switch to **Manual** once you understand levels

Setting Manual ovs audio levels (step by step)
If you choose **Manual**:

    Highlight **Rec. level**

    Press **SET**

    Use the **Rear Dial** to raise or lower the level

    Watch the audio meters on screen

    Aim for levels that peak below the red zone

    Press **SET** to confirm

On-screen behavior:

    Green bars = safe

    Yellow = getting loud

    Red = distortion (avoid this)

Audio meters: how to read them
While recording or monitoring:

    Audio meters appear on screen

    They move as sound enters the microphone

    If they hit red, sound is clipping

Best practice:

Normal speech should sit in the middle range

Avoid constant red peaks

Internal microphone behavior

The built-in microphone:

Is located on the camera body

Picks up sound from all directions

Also records handling noise and button presses

Important to know:

Image stabilization and autofocus noise may be recorded

Wind noise is common outdoors

Wind filter and attenuator

Inside the Sound recording menu, you may see:

Wind filter

Attenuator

Wind filter:

Reduces low-frequency wind noise

Useful outdoors

Can slightly affect voice tone

Attenuator:

Reduces very loud sounds

Useful for concerts or loud environments

Beginner advice:

Leave both OFF unless needed

Turn on Wind filter only outdoors

External microphone behavior

Photos and Videos Like a Pro

When you plug an external microphone into the **mic jack**:

>The camera automatically uses it

>The internal mic is disabled

>Audio quality improves significantly

Important camera-specific behavior:

>External mic levels are controlled in the same menu

>Manual level adjustment still applies

Always test audio before recording important clips.

Headphone monitoring (if available)
If headphones are connected:

>You can monitor audio in real time

>This helps catch noise or distortion early

How to use:

>Plug headphones into the headphone jack

>Adjust volume if available

>Listen while recording

How to confirm audio is being recorded
Before recording:

>Check audio meters are moving

>Confirm Sound recording is enabled

During recording:

>Audio meters continue moving

>No meters means no sound is being captured

After recording:

>Play back the clip

Confirm sound is present

Common beginner mistakes with audio

Forgetting Sound recording is disabled

Leaving levels too high

Ignoring audio meters

Relying only on the built-in mic

Not testing audio before recording

Best practice for beginners

Always switch to video mode first

Enable Sound recording

Start with Auto audio

Watch audio meters while recording

Use an external microphone when possible

Test a short clip before serious recording

Avoid touching the camera during recording

Audio quality on the Canon EOS R6 Mark III depends heavily on **correct menu setup**. Once you know where the controls are and how to read the meters, you can avoid silent or distorted video and produce clean, usable sound.

Microphone setup

Microphone setup on the Canon EOS R6 Mark III determines **where your audio comes from and how clean it sounds**. The camera can record sound using its **built-in microphone** or an **external microphone** connected to the mic input. Correct setup is essential before you press record.

This section explains **where the microphone input is**, **how to connect a microphone**, **how to confirm the camera is using it**, and **how to adjust levels**, step by step, in simple language.

Where the microphone jack is located

Hold the camera so you are looking at the **left side**

You will see a set of **rubber port covers**

Open the cover labeled for audio connections

Inside is the **3.5 mm microphone input jack**

This jack is used for external microphones only.

Using the built-in microphone

By default:

The camera uses the **internal microphone**

It records stereo sound

No setup is required

Important to understand:

It picks up **everything**, including:

Button presses

Handling noise

Lens and stabilization sounds

It is best for:

Casual clips

Reference audio

Quick recording

You do not need to enable anything special to use it.

Connecting an external microphone (step by step)

Turn the camera OFF

Open the **mic jack cover**

Plug the microphone's **3.5 mm cable** firmly into the mic jack

Make sure the plug is fully inserted

Turn the camera ON

Switch to **video mode**

Once connected:

The camera **automatically switches** to the external microphone

The internal microphone is disabled

No menu switch is required to select the external mic.

Mounting the microphone

Most external microphones are mounted on the camera.

Common mounting locations:

Hot shoe on top of the camera

Shock mount attached to the mic

Off-camera using a cable (for lavalier or boom mics)

Beginner advice:

Use a shock mount if possible

This reduces handling noise

Confirming the microphone is working

Before recording:

Switch to **video mode**

Press **MENU**

Go to **Red Movie Shooting tab**

Open **Sound recording**

Watch the **audio meters**

What to look for:

Meters should move when you speak

Movement confirms the mic is active

No movement means no sound is reaching the camera

Always test this before recording.

Setting audio levels for an external microphone

If using **Auto audio**:

The camera adjusts levels automatically

Good for beginners

Levels may change during recording

If using **Manual audio** (recommended for external mics):

Step-by-step:

Go to **Sound recording**

Set **Recording level** to **Manual**

Select **Rec. level**

Use the **Rear Dial** to adjust

Speak at normal volume

Watch the meters

Aim for strong green bars without hitting red

Press **SET** to confirm

This gives consistent, clean sound.

Wind filter and external microphones

When using an external microphone:

Wind filter affects only the audio signal

Some microphones already have wind protection

Best practice:

Turn OFF camera wind filter if the mic has a windscreen

Turn ON camera wind filter only if needed

Attenuator and loud environments

If recording very loud sound:

Enable **Attenuator** in Sound recording

This reduces signal strength

Prevents distortion

Use only when necessary.

Monitoring audio with headphones

If headphones are connected:

You can hear sound while recording

This helps catch issues early

How to use:

Plug headphones into the headphone jack

Start recording

Listen for distortion or noise

Always monitor audio for important recordings.

What happens if the microphone is unplugged during recording

Camera behavior:

Audio stops immediately

Recording continues silently

No warning sound is given

Always check cable connections before recording.

Common beginner mistakes with microphone setup

Plugging mic into the wrong port

Not fully inserting the mic plug

Forgetting to switch to video mode

Recording with Sound recording disabled

Not checking audio meters

Handling the camera during recording

Best practice for beginners

Always connect the microphone before recording

Switch to video mode first

Confirm meters are moving

Use Manual audio for external mics

Record a short test clip

Play it back and listen

Avoid touching the camera while recording

Microphone setup on the Canon EOS R6 Mark III is **automatic but not foolproof**. Once you know where the mic jack is and how to confirm audio input, you eliminate the most common cause of unusable video.

Overheating considerations

The Canon EOS R6 Mark III is a powerful video camera, but like all compact mirrorless cameras, it can **generate heat during long or demanding video recordings**. The camera is designed to protect itself automatically. Understanding how overheating works on this camera helps you **avoid interruptions and protect the hardware**.

This section explains **what causes heat, how the camera warns you, what happens when it gets hot**, and **how to manage heat properly**, step by step.

Why the R6 Mark III heats up during video
Heat builds up when:

Recording high-resolution video

Recording at high frame rates

Recording long continuous clips

Using advanced processing features

Writing large files continuously to the memory card

Video mode uses:

The sensor continuously

The image processor constantly

The memory card without breaks

This is normal behavior, not a fault.

How the camera monitors temperature
The R6 Mark III has **internal temperature monitoring**.

What the camera does:

Monitors internal heat levels

Predicts safe recording time

Adjusts behavior to protect itself

You do not need to enable this. It works automatically.

Overheating warning indicators
When heat increases:

A **temperature warning icon** appears on the screen

The icon may be yellow at first

It may turn red if temperature continues rising

This warning means:

The camera is getting hot

Recording time may be limited

You should prepare to stop recording

What happens if the camera gets too hot

If temperature reaches a critical level:

Video recording stops automatically

The camera may block new recordings

Some video options may become unavailable

This is a **safety shutdown**, not a crash.

The camera will not resume full operation until it cools down.

How overheating affects recording time

Camera-specific behavior:

Higher resolution = shorter safe recording time

Higher frame rate = shorter safe recording time

Longer continuous clips = faster heat buildup

Short clips:

Produce less heat

Allow the camera to cool between takes

What does NOT cause overheating

Important clarification:

Autofocus does not cause overheating

Audio recording does not cause overheating

Screen brightness has minimal effect

Still photography does not significantly heat the camera

Heat is mainly a **video recording issue**.

How to reduce overheating risk (practical steps)

Before recording:

Choose appropriate resolution and frame rate

Avoid unnecessary high settings

Use fast, reliable memory cards

During recording:

Record in shorter clips

Stop recording between takes

Avoid leaving the camera recording when not needed

Between recordings:

Turn the camera OFF

Let it sit idle

Open any port covers if safe to do so

Remove the battery briefly if needed

Environmental factors that increase heat

Be cautious when:

Shooting outdoors in hot weather

Shooting in direct sunlight

Recording in enclosed spaces

Using the camera on a tripod without airflow

Heat builds faster in warm environments.

How long cooling takes

Cooling time depends on:

- How hot the camera became

- Ambient temperature

- Whether the camera is powered off

Typical behavior:

- A few minutes may restore limited recording

- Full recovery may take longer

- The warning icon disappears when safe

Do not force recording while the warning is active.

Overheating and battery behavior

Camera-specific behavior:

- Heat affects battery performance

- Battery drains faster when the camera is hot

- Hot batteries recharge more slowly

If possible:

- Swap batteries

- Allow both camera and battery to cool

Common beginner mistakes related to overheating

- Ignoring the temperature warning icon

- Recording continuously without breaks

- Using highest video settings unnecessarily

- Thinking the camera is defective

- Restarting recording repeatedly when blocked

Best practice for beginners

- Start with moderate video settings

Record in short clips

Watch the temperature icon

Stop recording when warned

Let the camera cool naturally

Plan breaks during long video sessions

Do not panic when recording stops

Overheating protection on the Canon EOS R6 Mark III is a **built-in safety system**, not a limitation unique to your camera. When you understand how it works and plan your recording accordingly, you can shoot confidently without unexpected interruptions.

Beginner video settings
This section gives you a **safe, reliable starter setup** for recording video on the Canon EOS R6 Mark III. These settings are chosen to give **good image quality, stable autofocus, clean audio, and minimal overheating**, without requiring technical knowledge.

Follow these steps **in order**, exactly as written.

Step 1: Switch to video mode
Rotate the **Mode Dial** to the **movie camera icon**

Confirm video information appears on the screen

All video settings only apply after this step.

Step 2: Set video resolution and frame rate
Press **MENU**

Go to the **Red Movie Shooting tab**

Select **Movie recording quality**

Choose **Full HD 30p**

Press **SET**

Why this is best for beginners:

Good image quality

Smaller file sizes

Longer recording times

Less heat

Easy to edit

Step 3: Set exposure mode for video

Leave exposure control in **automatic video exposure**

Do not force Manual exposure yet

Why:

The camera handles brightness safely

Reduces beginner mistakes

Keeps exposure stable

Step 4: Set autofocus for video

Press **MENU**

Go to the **Purple Autofocus tab**

Set **Movie Servo AF** to **Enable**

Set **AF area** to **Whole area AF**

Set **Subject to detect** to **People**

Set **Eye detection** to **Enable**

Why this works:

Continuous focus during recording

Camera tracks faces automatically

Eye focus improves sharpness

Minimal manual intervention

Step 5: Enable Touch AF

Make sure **Touch AF** is enabled

Tap the screen to change focus targets if needed

This gives you control without pressing buttons.

Step 6: Set image look (Picture Style)

Press **MENU**

Go to **Picture Style**

Select **Standard**

Do not modify contrast or color tone

Why:

Natural colors

Ready-to-use video

No grading required

Step 7: Set white balance

Set **White Balance** to **Auto (AWB)**

Why:

Automatically adapts to lighting

Prevents color confusion

Best for mixed environments

Step 8: Set audio recording

Press **MENU**

Go to **Sound recording**

Set **Sound recording** to **Enable**

Set **Recording level** to **Auto**

Photos and Videos Like a Pro

Why:

Camera handles volume safely

Reduces clipping risk

Best for beginners

If using an external microphone:

Watch audio meters

Confirm movement before recording

Step 9: Stabilization

Leave stabilization **On** if available

Especially useful for handheld video

Why:

Reduces shake

Makes footage smoother

Helps beginners immediately

Step 10: Confirm before recording

Before pressing record, check:

Movie camera icon is visible

Resolution shows **Full HD 30p**

AF box is tracking faces

Audio meters are moving

No temperature warning icon

Step 11: Start recording

Press the **Record (video) button**

Do not press the shutter button

Watch the screen while recording:

AF box should stay on the subject

Audio meters should move

Recording timer should count up

Step 12: Stop recording

Press the **Record button again**

Wait for the camera to finish writing the file

Common beginner mistakes to avoid

Recording in photo mode

Using 4K before learning

Forgetting audio recording is disabled

Ignoring audio meters

Touching the camera during recording

Recording long clips without breaks

Best beginner workflow

Record short clips

Review playback immediately

Listen to audio

Check focus and exposure

Adjust only one setting at a time

Practice before important recordings

These beginner video settings turn the Canon EOS R6 Mark III into a **simple, dependable video camera** that works well without technical stress.

Chapter 2
Connectivity and Wireless Features

Wi-Fi setup

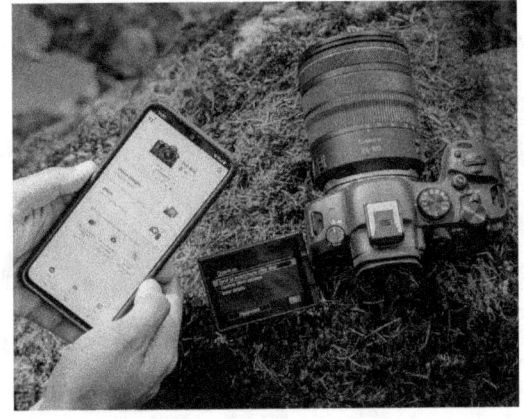

Wi-Fi on the Canon EOS R6 Mark III allows the camera to **connect wirelessly to a smartphone, tablet, or computer**. Once set up, you can transfer images, control the camera remotely, and share files without removing the memory card.

This section explains **where Wi-Fi settings are**, **how to turn Wi-Fi on**, and **how to complete the first connection**, step by step, in simple language.

Where Wi-Fi settings are located

All wireless controls are found in the **Setup Menu**, which appears as the **Yellow tab**.

Wi-Fi settings are available in both photo and video modes.

Turning Wi-Fi on (step by step)

Turn the camera ON

Press the **MENU** button

Navigate to the **Yellow Setup tab**

Scroll to **Wi-Fi / Bluetooth connection** or **Wireless communication**

   settings

Press **SET**

Select **Wi-Fi**

Set **Wi-Fi** to **Enable**

Press **SET** to confirm

When Wi-Fi is enabled:

A wireless icon may appear on the screen

The camera is ready to connect

First-time Wi-Fi setup behavior
The first time you enable Wi-Fi:

The camera may ask you to **set a nickname**

This name identifies your camera to other devices

How to set it:

Use the on-screen keyboard

Enter a simple name (for example, "R6MarkIII")

Press **SET** to confirm

You only do this once.

Choosing what to connect to
After enabling Wi-Fi:

The camera shows a **connection method screen**

Options may include:

Connect to smartphone

Connect to computer

Connect to printer

Select **Connect to smartphone**

Press **SET**

This is the most common beginner use.

Preparing your smartphone for connection

Before pairing:

Install Canon's official camera app on your phone

Turn ON Wi-Fi on your phone

Turn ON Bluetooth on your phone

Do not open other camera apps during setup.

Pairing the camera with a smartphone

On the camera:

Select **Connect to smartphone**

Choose **Add a device**

The camera displays connection instructions

On the phone:

Open the Canon camera app

Follow the on-screen steps

Select your camera when it appears

Approve the connection

On the camera:

A confirmation screen appears

Select **OK**

Press **SET**

The devices are now paired.

What happens after pairing

Once paired:

The camera remembers your phone

Future connections happen faster

Wi-Fi can reconnect automatically when needed

You do not need to repeat full setup every time.

Confirming Wi-Fi connection

You will know Wi-Fi is active when:

A wireless icon appears on the camera screen

The app shows the camera is connected

You can view images or control the camera from the phone

Turning Wi-Fi off when not needed

Wi-Fi uses battery power.

To turn it off:

Press **MENU**

Go to the **Yellow Setup tab**

Open **Wi-Fi / Bluetooth connection**

Set **Wi-Fi** to **Disable**

Press **SET**

Turn Wi-Fi off when not in use to save battery.

Common beginner mistakes with Wi-Fi setup

Forgetting to enable Wi-Fi in the menu

Not installing the correct camera app

Bluetooth turned off on the phone

Canceling pairing before confirmation

Leaving Wi-Fi on and draining the battery

Best practice for beginners

Enable Wi-Fi only when needed

Pair the camera once and reuse the connection

Keep the camera close to the phone during setup

Confirm connection before transferring images

Turn Wi-Fi off after use

Charge the battery before long wireless sessions

Wi-Fi setup on the Canon EOS R6 Mark III is **menu-based and beginner-friendly once you know where to look**. After the first pairing, wireless use becomes quick and reliable.

Bluetooth pairing

Bluetooth on the Canon EOS R6 Mark III is used for **low-power, always-on communication** between the camera and a smartphone. Unlike Wi-Fi, Bluetooth stays connected in the background and helps the camera **reconnect quickly**, transfer basic data, and enable remote functions smoothly.

This section explains **where Bluetooth settings are**, **how to pair the camera with a phone**, and **how Bluetooth behaves on this camera**, step by step.

What Bluetooth does on this camera

Maintains a constant low-power link to your phone

Helps Wi-Fi reconnect faster

Allows basic remote camera control

Enables location data sharing (if allowed)

Uses less battery than Wi-Fi

Bluetooth does not transfer large image files by itself. It works together with Wi-Fi.

Where Bluetooth settings are located

Bluetooth controls are found in the **Yellow Setup tab**, inside **Wi-Fi / Bluetooth connection**.

Bluetooth is available in both photo and video modes.

Turning Bluetooth on (step by step)

Turn the camera ON

Press the **MENU** button

Navigate to the **Yellow Setup tab**

Select **Wi-Fi / Bluetooth connection**

Press **SET**

Choose **Bluetooth settings**

Set **Bluetooth** to **Enable**

Press **SET** to confirm

A Bluetooth icon may appear on the screen once enabled.

Preparing your smartphone for Bluetooth pairing
Before pairing:

Install Canon's official camera app on your phone

Turn **Bluetooth ON** in your phone settings

Turn **Wi-Fi ON** in your phone settings

Keep the phone close to the camera

Do not connect the phone to other Bluetooth devices during pairing.

Pairing the camera with a smartphone (step by step)
On the camera:

In **Bluetooth settings**, select **Pairing**

Press **SET**

The camera waits for a device to connect

Photos and Videos Like a Pro

On the smartphone:

Open the Canon camera app

Follow the on-screen instructions

Select your camera when it appears

Approve the pairing request

On the camera:

A confirmation screen appears

Select **OK**

Press **SET**

Pairing is now complete.

What happens after Bluetooth pairing

Once paired:

The camera remembers the phone

Bluetooth reconnects automatically when both are on

Wi-Fi connections start faster when needed

The app can wake the camera remotely

You only need to pair once unless you reset settings.

Confirming Bluetooth connection

Bluetooth is active when:

A Bluetooth icon appears on the camera screen

The app shows the camera is connected

The camera appears as "paired" in the app

Bluetooth may stay connected even when Wi-Fi is off.

Using Bluetooth with Wi-Fi together

Camera-specific behavior:

Bluetooth handles background communication

Wi-Fi activates automatically when large transfers are needed

You do not need to manually switch each time

This makes wireless use smoother and faster.

Turning Bluetooth off
Bluetooth uses very little power, but you can disable it if needed.

To turn it off:

Press **MENU**

Go to the **Yellow Setup tab**

Open **Wi-Fi / Bluetooth connection**

Select **Bluetooth settings**

Set **Bluetooth** to **Disable**

Press **SET**

Disable Bluetooth if you want maximum battery savings.

Removing or changing a paired device
If you want to pair a new phone:

Open **Bluetooth settings**

Select **Paired devices**

Choose the current device

Select **Delete**

Confirm

You can then pair a new device.

Common beginner mistakes with Bluetooth pairing
Forgetting to enable Bluetooth in the camera menu

Bluetooth turned off on the phone

Closing the app during pairing

Pairing through phone settings instead of the camera app

Standing too far from the camera during setup

Best practice for beginners

Enable Bluetooth once and leave it on

Pair only through the official camera app

Use Bluetooth to speed up Wi-Fi connections

Turn off Bluetooth only if battery life is critical

Keep the camera nickname simple

Bluetooth pairing on the Canon EOS R6 Mark III is a **background convenience feature** that makes wireless use smoother and faster. Once paired, it quietly supports your workflow without constant setup.

Connecting to a smartphone

Connecting the Canon EOS R6 Mark III to a smartphone allows you to **transfer images and videos, control the camera remotely**, and **share files without removing the memory card**. This connection uses **Bluetooth for background pairing** and **Wi-Fi for data transfer**. Once set up the first time, reconnecting is quick and simple.

This section explains **exactly how to connect, what you see on the camera and phone**, and **how to confirm the connection is working**, step by step.

What you need before connecting

A smartphone (Android or iPhone)

Canon's official camera app installed on the phone

Bluetooth turned ON on the phone

Wi-Fi turned ON on the phone

Camera battery charged

Step 1: Turn on wireless functions on the camera

Turn the camera ON

Press the **MENU** button

Go to the **Yellow Setup tab**

Select **Wi-Fi / Bluetooth connection**

Press **SET**

Confirm **Bluetooth** is **Enable**

Confirm **Wi-Fi** is **Enable**

If this is your first time, the camera may ask for a nickname. Enter one and confirm.

Step 2: Choose smartphone connection on the camera

In **Wi-Fi / Bluetooth connection**

Select **Connect to smartphone**

Press **SET**

Choose **Add a device**

The camera displays connection instructions

Leave this screen open.

Step 3: Start connection from the smartphone

Open the Canon camera app on your phone

Follow the on-screen instructions

Select your camera when it appears

Approve Bluetooth pairing on the phone

Photos and Videos Like a Pro

The app will guide you automatically.

Step 4: Confirm pairing on the camera

On the camera screen:

    A confirmation message appears

    Select **OK**

    Press **SET**

Bluetooth pairing is now complete.

Step 5: Automatic Wi-Fi connection

After Bluetooth pairing:

    The camera automatically switches to Wi-Fi when needed

    You do not need to select a Wi-Fi network manually

    The phone and camera connect directly

This happens automatically in the background.

How to confirm the smartphone is connected

Connection is successful when:

    A wireless icon appears on the camera screen

    The app shows the camera as connected

    You can see image thumbnails on your phone

    Remote shooting becomes available

If these appear, the connection is active.

What you can do once connected

From the smartphone app, you can:

    View images and videos on the camera

    Transfer selected or all images

    Download files to the phone

Control the camera remotely

See live view from the camera

Trigger the shutter or start video recording

All of this works without touching the camera.

Reconnecting in the future

After the first setup:

Turn the camera ON

Open the camera app on the phone

The camera reconnects automatically

No need to repeat pairing unless settings are reset.

Disconnecting from the smartphone

To disconnect:

Close the app on the phone, or

Turn Wi-Fi/Bluetooth OFF in the camera menu, or

Turn the camera OFF

The connection ends safely.

Battery considerations

Wireless connections use power.

Best practice:

Turn Wi-Fi OFF when not needed

Leave Bluetooth ON for quick reconnection

Avoid long transfers on low battery

Common beginner mistakes

Forgetting to enable Wi-Fi in the camera menu

Pairing through phone Bluetooth settings instead of the app

Closing the app during setup

Standing too far from the camera

Expecting Bluetooth alone to transfer images

Best practice for beginners

Pair the camera once and reuse the connection

Always use the official Canon app

Keep phone and camera close during setup

Confirm connection icons before transferring files

Turn Wi-Fi off after use to save battery

Connecting the Canon EOS R6 Mark III to a smartphone is a **one-time setup that unlocks powerful wireless control**. Once paired, image transfer and remote shooting become fast and convenient.

Using Canon apps

Canon apps are the **official way to communicate with the Canon EOS R6 Mark III using a smartphone**. These apps allow you to connect, control, transfer, and manage images without removing the memory card. Everything is designed to work specifically with this camera once Wi-Fi and Bluetooth are set up.

This section explains **which Canon app to use**, **what each feature does**, and **how to use the app step by step**, in clear, beginner-friendly language.

Which Canon app to use

For the Canon EOS R6 Mark III, the primary and most important app is:

Canon Camera Connect

This is the app you should use as a beginner. It supports:

Wireless image transfer

Photos and Videos Like a Pro

Remote live view shooting

Video recording control

Camera settings access

Automatic reconnection using Bluetooth

Other Canon apps exist, but **Camera Connect is the core app** you need to learn first.

Installing the Canon Camera Connect app
On your smartphone:

Open your phone's app store

Search for **Canon Camera Connect**

Install the app

Allow permissions when prompted:

Bluetooth

Wi-Fi

Photos / Media

Location (optional)

Do not skip permissions, or features may not work.

Opening the app for the first time
Turn the camera ON

Make sure **Bluetooth and Wi-Fi are enabled** on the camera

Open **Canon Camera Connect** on your phone

The app will:

Search for nearby Canon cameras

Detect your R6 Mark III if paired

Ask for confirmation if needed

Photos and Videos Like a Pro

Once connected, the app shows the **main control screen**.

Main sections of the Canon Camera Connect app
When connected, you will see options such as:

Images on camera

Remote Live View Shooting

Camera settings

Auto transfer (if enabled)

Each option controls a specific function of the R6 Mark III.

Viewing images using the app
To view images on your phone:

Open the app

Tap **Images on camera**

Thumbnails of photos and videos appear

Tap an image to view it full size

From here, you can:

Swipe through images

Zoom in using pinch gestures

Select images to download

Images remain on the camera unless you delete them manually.

Transferring images to your phone
To transfer images:

Open **Images on camera**

Select one or more images

Tap **Download** or **Save to phone**

Wait for the transfer to complete

Photos and Videos Like a Pro

The app uses **Wi-Fi** for fast transfer.

Large files may take longer.

Remote live view shooting (very important feature)
This allows you to **see what the camera sees on your phone screen** and control the camera remotely.

To use it:

Open the app

Tap **Remote Live View Shooting**

The camera switches to remote control mode

Live view appears on your phone

You can now:

See real-time framing

Tap to focus

Change exposure settings

Press the shutter remotely

Start and stop video recording

This is ideal for:

Self-portraits

Group photos

Vlogging

Tripod shooting

Wildlife from a distance

Using touch focus from the app
While in Remote Live View:

Tap anywhere on the phone screen

The camera focuses on that area

Focus change is smooth and precise

This works just like Touch AF on the camera screen.

Starting video recording from the app

If the camera is in video mode:

Open **Remote Live View Shooting**

Frame your shot on the phone

Tap the **Record button** on the app

Tap again to stop recording

You do not need to touch the camera.

Camera settings control from the app

From the app, you may be able to:

Change shooting mode (limited)

Adjust exposure settings

Switch between photo and video

Control focus behavior

Not all settings are available, but the essentials are.

Automatic reconnection behavior

After first setup:

Bluetooth keeps a background connection

Opening the app reconnects automatically

Wi-Fi activates only when needed

You do not need to repeat pairing every time.

When the app will not connect

Common reasons:

Wi-Fi disabled on the camera

Bluetooth disabled on the phone

App permissions denied

Camera too far from the phone

Battery too low

Always check camera wireless settings first.

Battery considerations when using Canon apps
Using the app:

Drains camera battery faster

Drains phone battery as well

Best practice:

Use the app only when needed

Turn Wi-Fi off afterward

Carry spare batteries for long sessions

Common beginner mistakes
Installing the wrong Canon app

Trying to pair through phone Bluetooth settings

Closing the app during connection

Expecting Bluetooth alone to transfer images

Leaving Wi-Fi on all day

Best practice for beginners
Use **Canon Camera Connect only**

Pair the camera once and reuse

Use Remote Live View for tripod shots

Transfer only selected images

Turn Wi-Fi off after use

Keep firmware and app updated

Using Canon apps with the Canon EOS R6 Mark III turns your smartphone into a **remote control, monitor, and transfer hub**. Once you understand where each function is in the app, wireless shooting and sharing become simple and reliable.

Transferring photos and videos

Transferring photos and videos from the Canon EOS R6 Mark III to a smartphone is done using **Canon's official Camera Connect app**. The camera uses **Bluetooth to stay paired** and **Wi-Fi to move files**. You do not need to remove the memory card.

This section explains **where the transfer options are**, **how to transfer photos and videos step by step**, and **what to expect during the process**, in simple, beginner-friendly language.

What you need before transferring

Camera battery charged

Smartphone battery charged

Canon Camera Connect app installed

Bluetooth and Wi-Fi enabled on the phone

Wi-Fi and Bluetooth enabled on the camera

Camera and phone close to each other

Step 1: Turn on the camera and open the app

Turn the camera ON

Make sure the camera is not in sleep mode

Open **Canon Camera Connect** on your smartphone

Photos and Videos Like a Pro

If the camera was paired before, it will reconnect automatically.

Step 2: Confirm the camera is connected
Connection is confirmed when:

> The app shows the camera name

> A wireless icon appears on the camera screen

> The app displays main options like image viewing and remote
> shooting

If it does not connect:

> Check Wi-Fi and Bluetooth are enabled on both devices

> Keep the phone close to the camera

Step 3: Open images on the camera from the app

> In the app, tap **Images on camera**

> Wait while thumbnails load

> Photos and videos stored on the memory card appear on your phone
> screen

This does not delete anything from the camera.

Step 4: Transferring photos
To transfer photos:

> Tap the photo you want to transfer

> Tap **Download** or **Save to phone**

> Wait for the progress bar to complete

The photo is saved to your phone's gallery.

You can also:

> Select multiple photos

> Download them together in one action

Step 5: Transferring videos
Videos transfer the same way, but take longer.

To transfer a video:

  Tap the video thumbnail

  Tap **Download**

  Wait until transfer completes

Important to know:

  Large videos may take time

  Do not lock the phone screen during transfer

  Keep both devices close

Step 6: Choosing original size or reduced size
When transferring, the app may ask:

  Original size

  Reduced size

Original size:

  Best quality

  Larger file

  Slower transfer

Reduced size:

  Faster transfer

  Smaller file

  Good for social media

Choose based on how you plan to use the file.

Step 7: What happens after transfer
After transfer:

Files remain on the camera

Files are stored on the phone

No automatic deletion happens

You must delete images manually if you want to free space on the card.

Transferring while the camera is in playback mode

You can also initiate transfer while reviewing images:

Press **Playback**

Open the app

Select images

Download

Playback mode does not block transfers.

Auto image transfer behavior

If auto transfer is enabled:

Selected images may transfer automatically

Wi-Fi activates when needed

Battery drains faster

Most beginners should use **manual transfer**.

Where transferred files are stored on the phone

On most phones:

Photos go to the photo gallery

Videos go to the video folder

Files may appear in a Canon folder

Check your phone gallery if unsure.

Ending the transfer session

When finished:

Close the app, or

Turn Wi-Fi off in the camera menu, or

Turn the camera OFF

This saves battery.

Common beginner mistakes

Locking the phone during transfer

Walking too far from the camera

Expecting Bluetooth alone to transfer files

Transferring everything instead of selecting

Running out of battery mid-transfer

Best practice for beginners

Transfer only selected photos and videos

Use reduced size for quick sharing

Use original size for editing or backup

Keep devices close during transfer

Turn Wi-Fi off after finishing

Back up files before deleting anything

Transferring photos and videos from the Canon EOS R6 Mark III is **safe and straightforward once the connection is set up**. With a few taps, your images move from camera to phone without cables or card readers.

Remote shooting

Remote shooting on the Canon EOS R6 Mark III allows you to **control the camera from your smartphone without touching it**. You can see a live view, focus, take photos, and start or stop video recording directly from the phone using Canon's official app.

Photos and Videos Like a Pro

This feature is extremely useful for **self-portraits, group photos, tripod shots, vlogging, wildlife, and long exposures**.

This section explains **exactly how to start remote shooting**, **what controls are available**, and **how it behaves on this camera**, step by step.

What you need before remote shooting

Canon EOS R6 Mark III powered ON

Canon Camera Connect app installed

Camera already paired to the phone via Bluetooth

Wi-Fi enabled on the camera

Phone close to the camera

Step 1: Prepare the camera

Turn the camera ON

Place the camera on a tripod or stable surface

Choose **photo mode** or **video mode** on the camera using the Mode Dial

Make sure the lens cap is removed

Remote shooting follows whatever mode the camera is currently in.

Step 2: Open remote shooting in the app

Open **Canon Camera Connect** on your phone

Wait for the camera to connect

Tap **Remote Live View Shooting**

What happens on the camera:

The LCD may turn off or show a connection message

The camera switches to remote control mode

What happens on the phone:

Photos and Videos Like a Pro

A **live view feed** from the camera appears

You now see exactly what the camera sees

Step 3: Understanding the remote live view screen
On your phone screen you will see:

Live camera view

Shutter button (for photos)

Record button (for video)

Focus area indicator

Basic exposure controls

The phone becomes a **wireless monitor and controller**.

Step 4: Focusing using the phone
To focus:

Tap anywhere on the live view screen

What the camera does:

Focus moves to the tapped area

Autofocus activates just like Touch AF on the camera

Focus tracking continues if enabled

This works for faces, people, and detected subjects.

Step 5: Taking photos remotely
To take a photo:

Tap the **shutter button** on the phone

The camera captures the photo

The image is saved to the memory card

You may hear:

A shutter sound from the camera

Or see a shutter animation on the phone

The photo can then be transferred to the phone if desired.

Step 6: Recording video remotely
To record video:

Set the camera to **video mode** before opening remote shooting

In the app, tap **Remote Live View Shooting**

Tap the **Record button** on the phone

Tap again to stop recording

Important behavior:

Video records to the camera's memory card

Audio is captured by the camera, not the phone

Focus and exposure adjust automatically during recording

Step 7: Changing settings during remote shooting
While in remote live view, you can:

Change focus point by tapping

Adjust basic exposure controls

Switch between photo and video (limited)

Some advanced settings must still be changed on the camera.

Step 8: Ending remote shooting
To stop remote shooting:

Tap **Back** in the app, or

Close the app, or

Turn the camera OFF

The camera returns to normal operation immediately.

What remote shooting is best for

Photos and Videos Like a Pro

Self-portraits

Group photos

Tripod photography

Vlogging

Wildlife from a distance

Long exposures without camera shake

What remote shooting is not ideal for

Fast sports photography

Long-distance control

Situations with weak Wi-Fi signal

Battery considerations

Remote shooting uses:

Camera battery (Wi-Fi active)

Phone battery (live view streaming)

Best practice:

Use remote shooting only when needed

Turn Wi-Fi off afterward

Common beginner mistakes

Forgetting to set photo or video mode first

Expecting audio to record on the phone

Standing too far from the camera

Closing the app during recording

Forgetting to stop recording

Best practice for beginners

Always set shooting mode on the camera first

Photos and Videos Like a Pro

Use a tripod for stability

Tap to focus before taking the shot

Watch battery levels

Stop remote shooting when finished

Remote shooting on the Canon EOS R6 Mark III turns your smartphone into a **wireless control panel and live monitor**, making many types of photography and video much easier and more reliable.

Chapter 3
Customization and Personal Setup

Button customization

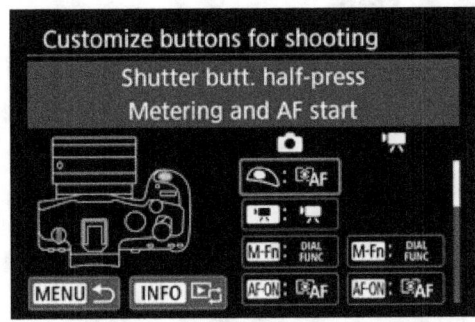

Button customization on the Canon EOS R6 Mark III allows you to **change what certain buttons and dials do**, so the camera matches **how you personally shoot**. This does not change image quality. It only changes **how quickly and comfortably you can access functions**.

This section explains **where button customization is located, how to assign functions, which buttons can be customized**, and **safe beginner choices**, step by step, in simple language.

What button customization does on this camera

Lets you assign frequently used functions to buttons

Reduces menu diving

Speeds up shooting

Makes the camera feel more personal

Button customization does not:

Damage the camera

Permanently lock settings

Affect image quality

You can reset everything at any time.

Where button customization is located

Photos and Videos Like a Pro

Button customization is found in the **Custom Functions Menu**, which appears as the **orange or custom tools tab** in the menu system.

Opening button customization (step by step)

Turn the camera ON

Press the **MENU** button

Navigate to the **Custom Functions / Custom Controls tab**

Select **Customize buttons** or **Custom controls**

Press **SET**

You are now on the button customization screen.

Understanding the button customization screen

On this screen:

You see a diagram or list of camera buttons

Each button has an assigned function

You can select any supported button and change its role

Buttons are shown exactly as they exist on the camera body.

Selecting a button to customize

Step-by-step:

Use the **Joystick** to highlight a button icon

Press **SET**

A list of assignable functions appears

Only compatible functions appear for each button.

Assigning a new function to a button

After selecting a button:

Scroll through the available functions

Highlight the function you want

Press **SET** to confirm

The button is reassigned immediately.

Buttons commonly available for customization

On the Canon EOS R6 Mark III, commonly customizable controls include:

AF-ON button

Shutter button half-press behavior

Control ring (if supported)

Rear buttons

Joystick press function

Video record button behavior (in some modes)

Not every button can be customized, and not all functions work on every button.

Safe beginner button customizations

If you are new, these are **low-risk, helpful choices**:

AF-ON button:

Assign **Autofocus activation**

Allows back-button focusing

Separates focus from the shutter

Joystick press:

Assign **Center AF point**

Quickly resets focus position

Video record button:

Keep default behavior until comfortable

Shutter button:

Leave default half-press focus and meter behavior

These changes improve control without confusion.

How customized buttons behave during shooting
Camera-specific behavior:

> Customized buttons work instantly

> The camera does not warn you during shooting

> The function changes apply immediately

> Behavior differs between photo and video modes

Always test buttons after customizing.

Customization differences between photo and video
Important to know:

> Photo mode and video mode may have **separate button behaviors**

> A button customized for photos may act differently in video

> Always check both modes if you shoot both

Resetting button customization
If something feels wrong:

> Press **MENU**

> Go to **Custom Functions / Custom Controls**

> Select **Clear all custom controls** or **Reset**

> Press **SET**

All buttons return to factory behavior.

Common beginner mistakes

> Customizing too many buttons at once

> Forgetting what was changed

> Assigning advanced functions too early

> Not testing after customization

Thinking customization is permanent

Best practice for beginners

Change one button at a time

Test the change immediately

Keep notes if needed

Use default settings at first

Customize only buttons you understand

Reset if confused

Button customization on the Canon EOS R6 Mark III is meant to **make the camera easier, not harder**. When done slowly and intentionally, it helps the camera adapt to you instead of the other way around.

Custom shooting modes

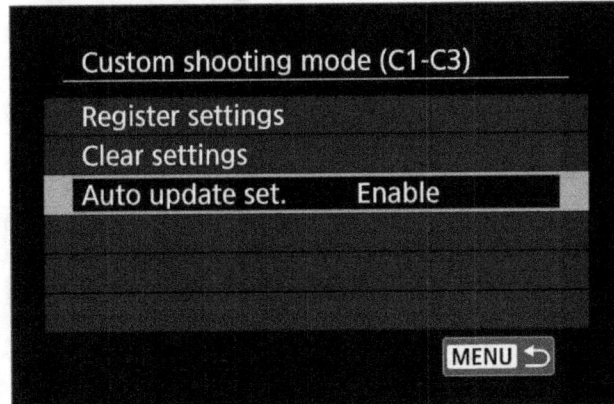

Custom shooting modes on the Canon EOS R6 Mark III allow you to **save a complete camera setup and recall it instantly** using the **Mode Dial**. These modes are labeled **C1, C2, and C3**. Each one can store how the camera is set up at that moment, including exposure, autofocus, drive mode, stabilization, and more.

This section explains **where Custom modes are**, **how to save settings to them**, **how to use them**, and **how they behave on this camera**, step by step, in simple language.

Where Custom shooting modes are located

Look at the **Mode Dial** on the **top of the camera**

You will see positions labeled:

C1

C2

C3

Turning the Mode Dial to any of these positions instantly loads the saved setup for that mode.

What a Custom mode actually saves

When you register a Custom mode, the camera stores:

Shooting mode (P, Av, Tv, M, or Auto video/photo behavior)

ISO setting

Aperture and shutter speed

Autofocus settings and AF area

Drive mode

Image stabilization state

White balance

Picture Style

Menu-based shooting options

Important to know:

It saves **how the camera is set at the moment of registration**

It does not update automatically unless you re-save it

How to set up the camera before saving a Custom mode

Before saving:

Turn the camera ON

Set the camera exactly how you want it to behave

Confirm all settings are correct

Test one photo or short clip if needed

Whatever you see now is what will be saved.

Registering settings to C1, C2, or C3 (step by step)

Press the **MENU** button

Navigate to the **Yellow Setup tab**

Scroll to **Custom shooting mode (C1–C3)** or **Register shooting mode**

Press **SET**

Choose **Register settings**

Select **C1**, **C2**, or **C3**

Press **SET** to confirm

The camera saves the current setup to that Custom mode.

Using a Custom shooting mode

To use a Custom mode:

Rotate the **Mode Dial**

Align it with **C1**, **C2**, or **C3**

Release the dial

What happens:

The camera instantly switches to the saved setup

No menu navigation is needed

The camera is ready to shoot immediately

What happens if you change settings while using a Custom mode

Camera-specific behavior:

If you change settings while in C1, C2, or C3:

The changes apply **temporarily**

If you turn the camera OFF or switch modes:

The camera returns to the saved version

To make changes permanent:

You must **re-register** the Custom mode

Updating a Custom mode

To update:

Turn the Mode Dial to the Custom mode you want to update

Change the camera settings as desired

Go back to **Register shooting mode**

Save again to the same C position

The old settings are replaced.

Clearing a Custom mode

If you want to remove saved settings:

Press **MENU**

Go to **Custom shooting mode**

Select **Clear settings**

Choose C1, C2, or C3

Confirm with **SET**

That Custom mode returns to default behavior.

Practical beginner examples for Custom modes

C1 – Everyday photography

Autofocus on

Stabilization on

Auto ISO

Standard Picture Style

C2 – Video recording

Video mode active

Movie Servo AF enabled

Audio recording enabled

Full HD video settings

C3 – Tripod or studio setup

Stabilization off

Manual exposure

Fixed ISO

Controlled focus behavior

These examples help you switch instantly without re-setting menus.

Common beginner mistakes

Forgetting to save after changing settings

Expecting Custom modes to auto-update

Overwriting a useful Custom mode by accident

Using Custom modes without testing

Not knowing which mode is currently active

Best practice for beginners

Use Custom modes only after learning basic controls

Label your Custom modes mentally (or in notes)

Save one purpose per Custom mode

Re-save whenever you intentionally change behavior

Test each Custom mode before important shoots

Reset if confused and start again

Custom shooting modes on the Canon EOS R6 Mark III are a **powerful time-saving tool**. Once you understand how to save and recall them, you can switch shooting styles instantly without touching the menu.

My Menu setup

My Menu on the Canon EOS R6 Mark III lets you create a **personal shortcut menu** containing only the items you use most. Instead of searching through many menu tabs, you can place your favorite settings in one place and access them quickly.

This section explains **where My Menu is**, **how to add items**, **how to organize them**, and **how to use My Menu day to day**, step by step, in simple language.

What My Menu does on this camera

Creates a custom menu page just for you

Holds shortcuts to frequently used settings

Reduces menu scrolling

Works in both photo and video modes

Can be edited or cleared at any time

My Menu does not change how settings work. It only changes **how fast you can reach them**.

Where My Menu is located

Press **MENU**

Scroll to the **Green tab** labeled **My Menu**

This tab appears at the **far right** of the menu system

If My Menu is empty, it will show setup options.

Opening My Menu for the first time

Press **MENU**

Navigate to the **Green My Menu tab**

Select **Configure**

Press **SET**

You are now in the My Menu configuration screen.

Adding items to My Menu (step by step)

In the **My Menu configuration** screen, select **Add items**

Press **SET**

A full list of menu categories appears

Choose the menu tab where the item lives (Shooting, AF, Playback,

Setup, etc.)

Press **SET**

Scroll to the specific menu item you want

Press **SET** to add it

The item is added to My Menu immediately.

What kinds of items you can add

You can add most menu items, including:

Image stabilization settings

ISO settings

White balance

Autofocus options

Audio recording settings

Movie recording quality

Wi-Fi / Bluetooth controls

Card formatting

Custom controls

You cannot add:

Live view screens

Buttons themselves

Some system-only functions

Viewing and using My Menu

Once items are added:

Press **MENU**

Go to the **Green My Menu tab**

You will see a list of your chosen items

Select any item

Press **SET** to open it directly

This works exactly like opening the item from its original location.

Reordering items in My Menu

To change the order:

Open the **Green My Menu tab**

Select **Configure**

Choose **Sort**

Press **SET**

Highlight an item

Move it up or down using the joystick or dials

Press **SET** to confirm placement

Put your most-used items at the top.

Removing items from My Menu

To remove an item:

Open **My Menu**

Select **Configure**

Choose **Delete items**

Highlight the item you want to remove

Press **SET**

Confirm deletion

The original menu item remains unchanged.

Clearing My Menu completely

If you want to start over:

Open **My Menu**

Select **Configure**

Choose **Clear all items**

Press **SET**

Confirm

My Menu becomes empty again.

Showing My Menu first when pressing MENU

You can make My Menu appear immediately when you press MENU.

To enable this:

Open **My Menu**

Select **Configure**

Turn **Display My Menu first** to **Enable**

Press **SET**

Now:

Pressing MENU opens My Menu first

You save time on every menu access

This is highly recommended for beginners.

Practical beginner My Menu suggestions

Good starter items to add:

> Image stabilization
>
> ISO settings
>
> White balance
>
> Movie recording quality
>
> Sound recording
>
> Wi-Fi / Bluetooth connection
>
> Format card
>
> Autofocus operation

These cover common adjustments without confusion.

Common beginner mistakes

> Adding too many items
>
> Forgetting what was added
>
> Not enabling "Display My Menu first"
>
> Using My Menu before understanding the settings
>
> Forgetting My Menu exists

Best practice for beginners

> Add only 5–8 frequently used items
>
> Group related items together
>
> Put emergency items like Format at the bottom
>
> Enable "Display My Menu first"
>
> Update My Menu as your skills grow
>
> Clear and rebuild if it becomes messy

My Menu on the Canon EOS R6 Mark III is a **personal control center**. Once set up properly, it saves time, reduces stress, and makes the camera feel simpler and faster to use.

Saving preferred settings

Saving preferred settings on the Canon EOS R6 Mark III allows you to **lock in the way you like your camera to behave**, so you do not need to repeat the same setup every time you turn it on or switch shooting styles. This is different from temporary changes. These settings are **intentionally stored and can be recalled reliably**.

This section explains **what can be saved**, **where saving is done**, and **how to save your preferred setup step by step**, in a clear, beginner-friendly way.

What "saving preferred settings" means on this camera

On the R6 Mark III, saving preferred settings usually means one of three things:

Registering settings to **Custom shooting modes (C1, C2, C3)**

Making sure default power-on behavior matches your preference

Keeping menu and control customizations consistent

The most reliable and beginner-safe method is **saving to Custom shooting modes**, because they preserve a complete setup.

Preparing the camera before saving settings

Before saving anything:

Turn the camera ON

Set the camera exactly how you like it

Confirm all important settings are correct

Photos and Videos Like a Pro

This includes:

Photo or video mode

Exposure mode (P, Av, Tv, M)

ISO behavior

Autofocus settings

Drive mode

Image stabilization state

White balance

Picture Style

Audio settings (for video)

The camera saves **what it sees right now**, so preparation is critical.

Saving preferred settings to a Custom mode (step by step)
This is the main method.

Press the **MENU** button

Go to the **Yellow Setup tab**

Scroll to **Custom shooting mode (C1–C3)** or **Register shooting mode**

Press **SET**

Select **Register settings**

Choose **C1**, **C2**, or **C3**

Press **SET** to confirm

Your current camera setup is now saved.

Using your saved preferred settings
To recall saved settings:

Rotate the **Mode Dial** on top of the camera

Turn it to **C1**, **C2**, or **C3**

86

Release the dial

The camera immediately switches to your saved preferences.

No menus are required.

Understanding how saved settings behave

Important camera-specific behavior:

Changes made while using C1, C2, or C3 are **temporary**

Turning the camera OFF resets the mode back to the saved version

Switching to another mode and back reloads the saved settings

If you want changes to be permanent:

You must **re-register** the Custom mode

Updating saved preferred settings

To update:

Switch the Mode Dial to the Custom mode you want to update

Adjust the camera to your new preferred settings

Go back to **Register shooting mode**

Save again to the same C position

The old settings are replaced.

Saving preferences without Custom modes

Some preferences remain active without Custom modes, such as:

My Menu layout

Button customization

Menu display behavior

Wireless pairing information

These stay saved until you reset the camera.

When to save preferred settings

Save preferred settings when:

- You like how the camera behaves

- You have tested the setup

- You use the same setup often

- You want quick access without menu changes

Do not save settings you are still experimenting with.

Beginner examples of preferred settings to save

Example 1: Everyday photography

- Autofocus enabled

- Stabilization ON

- Auto ISO

- Standard Picture Style

Save to C1.

Example 2: Video recording

- Video mode active

- Movie Servo AF ON

- Audio recording ON

- Full HD video settings

Save to C2.

Example 3: Tripod shooting

- Stabilization OFF

- Manual exposure

- Fixed ISO

Save to C3.

Common beginner mistakes

Saving before checking all settings

Forgetting which Custom mode holds what

Expecting Custom modes to update automatically

Overwriting a useful setup accidentally

Saving experimental settings too early

Best practice for beginners

Save only tested setups

Assign one purpose per Custom mode

Re-save intentionally after changes

Keep notes on what each Custom mode does

Reset and rebuild if things feel confusing

Use Custom modes as your main "memory system"

Saving preferred settings on the Canon EOS R6 Mark III turns the camera into a **predictable, personal tool**. Once saved correctly, the camera behaves the way you expect every time you switch it on.

Chapter 4
Maintenance and Care

Cleaning the camera body

Keeping the Canon EOS R6 Mark III clean helps it work properly and last longer. Cleaning the body is safe if done gently and correctly.

Where dirt usually collects:

Hand grip and rear buttons

Top dials and Mode Dial

LCD screen and viewfinder eyecup

Ports and rubber covers

How to clean the camera body step by step:

Turn the camera OFF

Remove the lens

Close all port covers

Use a soft, dry microfiber cloth

Gently wipe the camera surfaces

Use a blower to remove dust from seams and buttons

Important rules:

Do not use water or liquid cleaners

Do not spray air directly into buttons

Do not use alcohol or household wipes

Do not press hard on buttons or dials

For stubborn dirt:

Lightly dampen the cloth with clean water

Wipe gently

Dry immediately with a dry cloth

Cleaning the sensor

The sensor is inside the camera and is exposed **only when the lens is removed**. Dust on the sensor can appear as dark spots in photos, especially against bright backgrounds.

When sensor cleaning is needed:

You see repeating dark spots in images

Spots appear in the same place on multiple photos

Spots are visible at smaller apertures

Using the built-in sensor cleaning system:

Turn the camera ON

Press **MENU**

Go to the **Yellow Setup tab**

Select **Sensor cleaning**

Choose **Clean now**

Press **SET**

The camera vibrates the sensor to shake off dust.

Manual sensor cleaning (advanced):

Only attempt this if you are confident

Use a blower designed for camera sensors

Never touch the sensor with fingers

Never use compressed air cans

If dust remains:

Take the camera to a professional service center

Do not scrape or wipe the sensor yourself

Best beginner advice:

>Rely on automatic sensor cleaning

>Avoid changing lenses in dusty places

>Point the camera downward when changing lenses

Battery care
Proper battery care ensures reliable performance and long battery life.

Charging the battery:

>Use the official charger or supported USB-C charging

>Insert the battery correctly

>Do not force the battery into the charger

>Remove the battery once fully charged if possible

Using the battery:

>Avoid fully draining the battery often

>Recharge before it reaches zero

>Keep spare batteries for long sessions

Heat and battery safety:

>Do not leave batteries in direct sunlight

>Do not charge hot batteries

>Let batteries cool before charging

>Remove the battery if the camera becomes very hot

Long-term battery care:

>If not using the camera for weeks, store batteries partially charged

>Do not store batteries completely empty

>Check stored batteries every few months

Storage tips

Proper storage protects the camera when it is not in use.

Short-term storage:

> Turn the camera OFF
>
> Remove the lens if not in use
>
> Attach the body cap
>
> Store in a clean, dry place

Long-term storage:

> Remove the battery
>
> Remove the memory cards
>
> Store the camera in a padded camera bag
>
> Use silica gel packs to reduce moisture

Environmental considerations:

> Avoid humid environments
>
> Avoid extreme heat or cold
>
> Do not store the camera in a car
>
> Keep away from dust and sand

Lens storage tips:

> Attach lens caps
>
> Store lenses upright if possible
>
> Avoid stacking heavy items on lenses

Before using the camera after storage:

> Reinsert the battery
>
> Check for dust
>
> Power on and test basic functions

Clean exterior if needed

Common beginner mistakes in maintenance

Cleaning with rough cloths

Touching the sensor

Using household cleaning sprays

Leaving batteries fully drained

Storing the camera in humid places

Best practice for beginners

Clean gently and regularly

Use the built-in sensor cleaning first

Handle batteries with care

Store the camera dry and protected

When unsure, do less—not more

Seek professional cleaning if needed

Proper maintenance and care keep the Canon EOS R6 Mark III **reliable, clean, and ready to shoot** whenever you need it. Simple habits make a big difference over time.

Chapter 5

Common Problems and Simple Fixes

This chapter helps you quickly solve the **most common issues beginners face** with the Canon EOS R6 Mark III. Each problem is explained in plain language, with **camera-specific checks** you can perform immediately.

Camera won't turn on

If the camera does not power up, work through these steps in order.

Check the power switch

Confirm the **power switch** (around the Mode Dial area) is fully set to

ON

Do not leave it halfway between positions

Check the battery

Open the **battery compartment** on the bottom of the camera

Remove the battery and reinsert it firmly

Make sure the battery is inserted in the correct orientation

Check battery charge

If the battery is low or empty, the camera will not turn on

Charge the battery fully using the official charger or USB-C power

Check the battery door

The camera will not power on if the battery door is not fully closed

Close it until it clicks into place

Check temperature

If the camera is very hot or very cold, it may delay powering on

Let it return to normal room temperature

If none of the above works

> Remove the battery for one minute

> Reinsert and try again

> If the camera still does not turn on, professional service may be required

Autofocus not working

If the camera refuses to focus or keeps hunting, the cause is usually a setting.

Check lens focus mode

> Look at the **lens barrel**

> Make sure the switch is set to **AF**, not **MF**

Check AF operation setting

> Press **MENU**

> Go to the **Purple Autofocus tab**

> Confirm **AF operation** is enabled (One-Shot, Servo, or Movie Servo depending on mode)

Check AF area

> If AF is set to a very small point, the camera may miss the subject

> Switch to **Whole area AF** for beginners

Check subject detection

> If Subject detection is ON but no subject is present, AF may hesitate

> Try switching Subject detection to **None** temporarily

Check light conditions

> Autofocus needs contrast

> In very low light or on plain surfaces, AF may struggle

Aim at an edge or textured area

Check mode

Make sure you are not in a mode that limits autofocus behavior

Confirm whether you are in **photo mode** or **video mode**, as AF

settings differ

Blurry photos

Blurry photos usually come from **camera movement, subject movement,**

or focus issues.

Check shutter speed

Slow shutter speeds cause blur when handheld

Use a faster shutter speed or enable stabilization

Check stabilization

Confirm **In-body IS** is ON for handheld shooting

Confirm **Lens IS** is ON if the lens has an IS switch

Check focus confirmation

Make sure the focus box turns green or confirms focus before taking

the shot

Do not press the shutter fully before focus locks (unless using Servo

AF)

Check subject movement

If the subject is moving, blur may still happen

Use faster shutter speeds or continuous AF

Check handholding technique

Hold the camera firmly with both hands

Keep elbows close to your body

Press the shutter gently

Tripod situation

If using a tripod, turn stabilization OFF

Stabilization can cause blur on a tripod

Overexposed or underexposed images

If images look too bright or too dark, exposure settings are the cause.

Check exposure compensation

Look for the **± exposure scale** on screen

If it is set to + or − values, reset it to 0

Check metering

Extreme lighting can confuse metering

Reframe or change metering mode if needed

Check ISO

Very high ISO can brighten images unexpectedly

Use Auto ISO or lower ISO in bright light

Check shooting mode

In Manual (M) mode, exposure will not adjust automatically

Switch to P, Av, or Tv if you want the camera to help

Check white or black scenes

Bright scenes (snow, sky) may look underexposed

Dark scenes may look overexposed

Use exposure compensation gently rather than drastic changes

Video issues

If video does not record correctly, review these common fixes.

Video won't start recording

Photos and Videos Like a Pro

    Confirm the **Mode Dial** is set to the **movie camera icon**

    Press the **Record button**, not the shutter button

No sound in video

    Press **MENU**

    Go to **Sound recording**

    Confirm **Sound recording** is set to **Enable**

    Check that audio meters move

Video stops recording unexpectedly

    The camera may be managing heat

    Reduce resolution or frame rate

    Allow the camera to cool before continuing

Autofocus hunting during video

    Enable **Movie Servo AF**

    Use **Whole area AF**

    Reduce AF tracking sensitivity if needed

Shaky video

    Enable **In-body IS**

    Enable **Lens IS** if available

    Hold the camera steady or use a tripod

Video looks too dark or bright

    Exposure settings may be locked

    Check exposure compensation

    Confirm you are not in a restrictive manual setup

Common beginner troubleshooting mistakes

    Changing many settings at once

Forgetting which mode the camera is in

Ignoring on-screen icons and warnings

Assuming the camera is faulty instead of checking settings

Best practice for solving problems

Stop and check one thing at a time

Confirm shooting mode first

Confirm lens switches second

Confirm menu settings third

Test with one photo or short clip

Reset settings if confusion continues

Most issues on the Canon EOS R6 Mark III are **setting-related, not hardware failures**. Once you know where to look and what to check, problems are usually solved in minutes.

.